SPIRAL

GUIDE

MEXICO

D0586876

AA
Publishing

Contents

the magazine 5

Written by Robin Barton

Verified by Anto Howard

Project editor Karen Kemp
Designer Alan Gooch
Cartographic editor Anna Thompson
Managing editor Clare Garcia

Published by AA Publishing, a trading name of Automobile
Association Developments Limited, whose registered office is
Fanum House, Basing View, Basingstoke, Hampshire, RG21 4EA.
Registered number 1878835.

ISBN: 978-0-7495-5556-6

The contents of this publication are believed correct at the time
of printing. Nevertheless, AA Publishing accept no responsibilty
for errors, omissions or changes in the details given, or for the
consequences of readers' reliance on this information. This does
not affect your statutory rights. Assessments of the attractions,
hotels and restaurants are based upon the author's own experience
and contain subjective opinions that may not reflect the publisher's
opinion or a reader's experience. We have tried to ensure accuracy,
but things do change, so please let us know if you have any com-
ments or corrections.

A CIP catalogue record for this book is available from the
British Library.

Cover design and binding style by permission of AA Publishing

Colour separation by Keenes, Andover
Printed and bound in China by Leo Paper Products

Find out more about AA Publishing and the wide range of services
the AA provides by visiting our website at www.theAA.com/travel

A03007
Maps in this title produced from:
mapping © MAIRDUMONT/Falk Verlag 2007
and map data © Footprint Handbooks Limited 2004

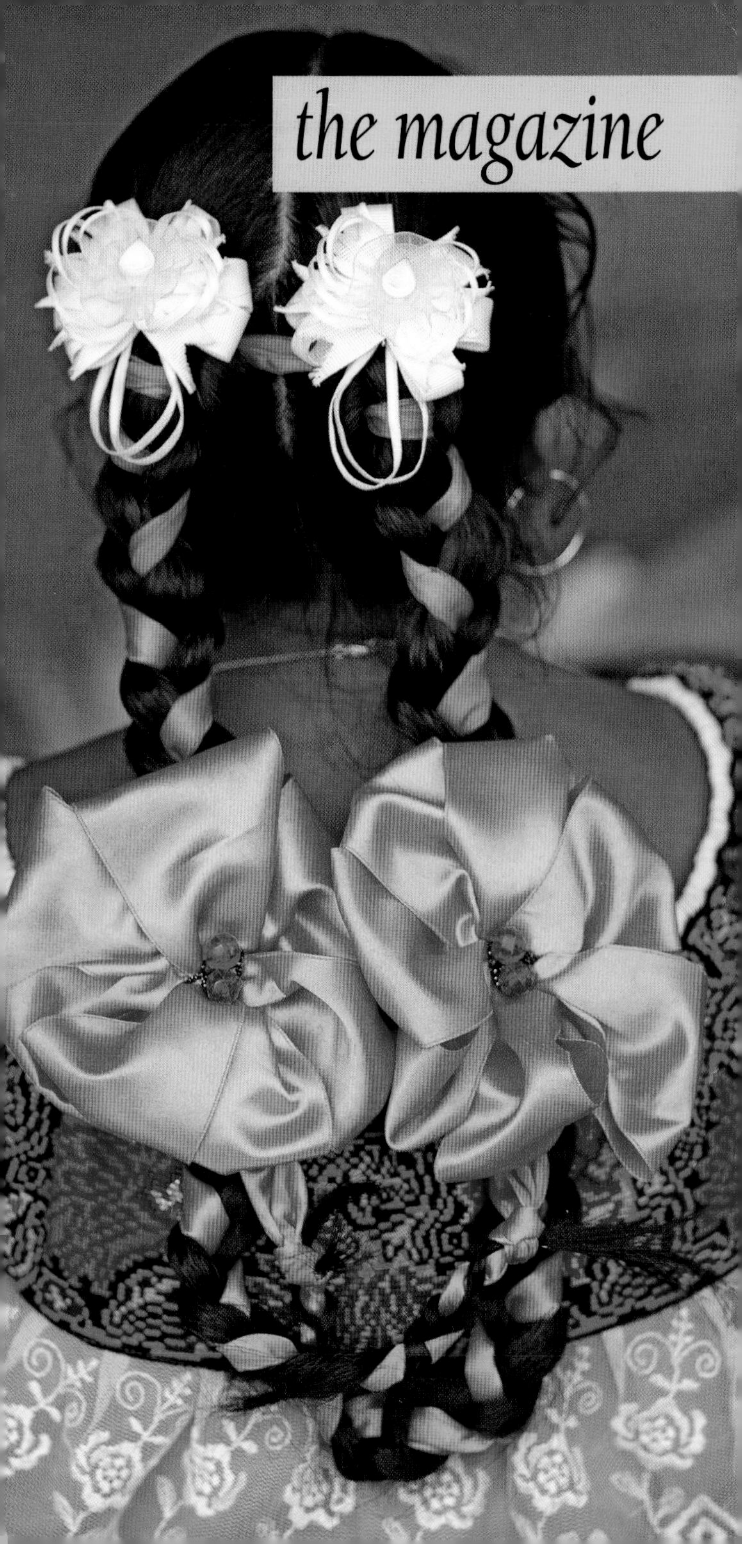
the magazine

THE PYRAMIDS

Nobody is quite sure why early Mexican civilizations built the number of pyramids that have been discovered all over the country. Some are built over burial tombs, while others appear to be central to ceremonies and sacrificial rituals. One thing is certain: the pyramid was the most important construction in their civilizations and they are no less enthralling today.

Teotihuacán and Chichén Itzá

Mexico boasts the biggest and most complex examples of pyramid building in the world. The largest, the Pirámide de Sol (Pyramid of the Sun) at Teotihuacán, has a floor area of 46,000sq m (55,000sq yards) and was built between AD 100 and 400, a time when this vast site was becoming an empire that rivaled Rome's in scale. The civilization was crumbling by AD 650 but the pyramid, and its partner, the Pirámide de la Luna (Pyramid of the Moon), remain.

Inset: The view across Teotihuacán from the Pyramid of the Moon

Chichén Itzá, in the Yucatán, recently named one of the "new seven wonders of the world," is the most famous of the Mayan pyramids, and holds further astronomical secrets, representing the Mayan calendar in the number of steps and panels in its design. It is now a must-see stop on any tour of the Yucatán's Mayan ruins.

Ritual Killings

But while sightseers clamber over the ruins, archaeologists are still trying to piece together the complete picture of how and why these pyramids were constructed. Many Mayan sites have yet to be rescued from the jungle that has enveloped them over the centuries and they too will reveal further secrets.

In 2006 it was discovered that people and wild animals were ritually killed or buried alive in the foundations of Teotihuacán's Pyramid of the Moon as a way of consecrating the pyramid. And in the same year a 1500-year-old pyramid was discovered under the outskirts of Mexico City.

Above: Temple of the Inscriptions, Palenque

Left: The ruined palace of Hachakum, Yaxchilán, with its distinctive roofcomb crowning the top

The Mexican authorities have been careful to protect the country's heritage, and the sites of the most popular ruins – including Chichén Itzá, Uxmal and Teotihuacán – are generally well managed, but it's always a good idea to visit them as early as possible in the day to avoid the crowds and the sometimes intense heat of midday.

If you get the chance, seek out some of the less well-known ruins, such as magical Palenque and Yaxchilán in the south of the country. In these places, where you might share an early morning walk with just a handful of people and a cacophony of birdsong, the impact of the pyramids and temples seems to be all the greater.

A TASTE OF MEXICO

**Below left to right: Hot jalapeno peppers; prickly pear cactus; edible grasshoppers; fast-food Mexico style
Bottom: Tequila**

Mexican food has the reputation of having all the subtlety of a tequila slammer – it's assumed by many first-time visitors to be fried, eye-wateringly hot or coated in cheese or all three. But while Mexican street food – *tacos*, *burritos*, *enchiladas* and *chile rellenos* – is never going to qualify as fine dining, the reality is that Mexican cuisine is far more varied and subtle than it is often given credit for. True, the flavors tend to be big and bold, but for anyone with an interest in food, Mexico will be a thoroughly delicious experience.

Staple Diet

Corn has long been a staple of Mexican cooking, with flat pancakes forming the basis of *enchiladas* and *tacos*. Indeed, corn was an important part of pre-Hispanic Mexican mythology and there was even a god of corn. Another source of carbohydrate is the black or pinto bean, often refried and served daily at all three meals. Adding flavor to this base are chilis, fruits (such as avocado for guacamole) and spices. While Mexican food is thought to be hot, you'll find that many of the hottest parts of the meal are the dips, which are optional.

Meat

There are also significant regional variations. *Carne asado* (grilled meat) is a staple of the ranching country of northern Mexico, while in the tropical Yucatán pork is marinaded in Seville

orange juice (or lemon and lime) to create the classic dish *cochinita pibil*, served in a banana leaf.

Seafood comes in a wide range of styles along the Caribbean and Pacific coasts.

In the cities and upscale tourist spots, a new restaurant movement is introducing a style described as *alta cocina Mexicana* to discerning diners: the portions are smaller, but the flavors are more distinct.

Desserts

Mexicans also have a sweet tooth; breakfast may simply be a sugary pastry while desserts tend to be very sweet. Flan, egg custard with caramel sauce, the equivalent of a creme caramel, and *churros*, like donuts, but in a long stick, are popular. And we have the Mexicans to thank for chocolate, which was first prepared as a drink flavored with cocoa beans and vanilla by the Aztecs.

Below left to right: Mexican beer (*cerveza*); fish in spicy red chili sauce; unusual fruit from Ocosingo; tacos (flour tortillas with meat sauce); mangoes; fresh fruit platter; beer and colorful cocktails; cocoa pod

Tequila and Mescal

If tequila is a fiery drink, its country cousin mescal is positively explosive. Tequila and mescal are both made from variants of the *agave*, a spiky plant from the family of succulents that is often seen planted in rows in field after field. While tequila comes from the blue *agave* plant and is distilled in Jalisco state, mescal has its roots in Oaxaca state and comes from the fleshy heart of the plant, which is roasted, crushed, fermented and distilled to produce the rough-edged spirit. Tequila is closely associated with nights out that are difficult to recall afterwards, and a pounding headache. However, try a fine, aged tequila and a whole new world opens up. The best tequilas are up to 15 years old and are never drunk with lime or salt, which are used to disguise the taste of cheap tequilas. Nor should a worm be in the bottle; this was a marketing gimmick when the drink was introduced to the United States. In Oaxaca, mescal aficionados ascribe a similar complexity to the spirit – there are *joven* (young, or white) mescals all the way up to *gran reserva* mescals (aged for a minimum of five years). The taste should be smoky but not fiery.

HOME-GROWN TALENT

Mexican cinema has come a long way since the 1960s and 1970s when the desert around Durango (► 72) stood in for the Wild West in films such as Sam Peckinpah's *Pat Garrett and Billy the Kid* (1973). Today, Mexican actors and directors are fêted by Hollywood and the range of movies produced in Mexico or with Mexican talent has expanded to include road movies, horror films, love stories and sophisticated dramas such as the 2006 Oscar-nominated film *Babel*, directed by Alejandro González Inárritu.

Inárritu, one of the leading lights of the new wave of Mexican cinema, was born in Mexico City in 1963. He came to the attention of Hollywood with the fast-paced drama *Amores Perros* (*Love's a Bitch*), which followed three interwoven stories, all connected to a car crash in Mexico City. The film's Mexican cast included Gael García Bernal, who has also moved onto the Hollywood A-list.

But back to Inárritu. After *Amores Perros* was released in 2000, Inárritu was offered the Hollywood-funded film *21 Grams*, another drama, this time featuring well-known names such as Sean Penn and Naomi Watts. *Babel*, starring Brad Pitt and Cate Blanchett, followed *21 Grams*.

After hitting the headlines with his performance in *Amores Perros*, Guadalajara-born García Bernal's next job was in *Y Tu Mamá También* (*And Your Mother Too*), a warmly received coming-of-age movie also set in Mexico. It was directed by Mexican filmmaker Alfonso Cuarón. Bernal's role in *Y Tu Mamá También* brought him to the attention of Hollywood's casting directors. The London-trained actor was selected to play Che Guevara in the biopic *The Motorcycle Diaries* (2004).

The success of *Y Tu Mamá También* also brought Alfonso Cuarón into the mainstream and he accepted the job of directing the third instalment of the Harry Potter movies, *Harry Potter and the Prisoner of*

Above: Alejandro González Inárritu

Right: Gael García Bernal

Below: Villa del Oeste film set, Durango